The Best Of BritCit!

Welcome to the **1993 Judge Dredd Yearbook** which takes the Britain of Dredd's future as its theme. Every story features an element of Brit-Cit - some feature the future Britain as their setting, others have Brit-Cit villains, some star Brit-Cit judges. All of which raises the obvious question - why choose Brit-Cit as the theme?

Several new stories and characters based in Brit-Cit have appeared in **Judge Dredd The Megazine** and **2000 AD** in the last two years - among them Armitage, Judge Joyce, Brit-Cit Babes and the Soul Sisters. These stories have begun to explore a part of Dredd's world long hinted but rarely seen. Indeed, the first Brit-Cit judge did not appear in **2000 AD** until the story *Judge Dredd: Atlantis* in prog 485 in August 1986 - nearly 10 years after the first Dredd story!

Now Brit-Cit is finally getting the attention it deserves and this whole Yearbook devoted to Brit-Cit, with stories about its perps and perculiarities. For more about the characters in this mighty volume, make sure you buy **2000 AD** every week and **Judge Dredd The Megazine** every fortnight - missing an issue of either would be a crime! Now enjoy this Yearbook, creeps - and that's an order!

COVER ART: Brendan McCarthy

EDITOR: David Bishop
DESIGNER: Sean Phillips
DTP WIZARD: Dominic Gregory
MANAGING EDITOR: Steve MacManus
MANAGING DIRECTOR: Jon Davidge

Published by Fleetway Editions Ltd., Greater London House, Hampstead Road, London NW1 7QQ. Judge Dredd Yearbook 1993 must not be sold at more than the recommended selling price shown on the cover. All rights reserved and reproduction without prior permission strictly forbidden. Origination by Colour Response Ltd, London. Printed by Casterman S.A., Belgium.

£5.95

TUM TE TUM...

HUM DE HEE...

OH MY GRUD!

FIFTY THREE!

BE WITH YOU IN A SECOND, DEAR.

AMPEY QUESTIONED THE WITNESSES. TWO CITIZENS SAY THEY SAW A SMALL MAN IN A LONG COAT AND DARK GOGGLES SKULKING FROM THE WAITING ROOM. THAT'S IT. EVERYONE ELSE BLIND AS USUAL.

NOT MUCH TO GO ON.

THE HOV STOP IS FORTY KAYS FROM HERE. THE KILLER'S GOT TO BE AIRBORNE, WE KNOW THAT.

GET EVERY AVAILABLE UNIT ON IT. WE'VE GOT **TWENTY SEVEN** DEAD SO FAR AND MORE TO COME. WE CAN BE PRETTY SURE THIS CREEP'S GOING FOR THE **RECORD**.

HUNT

THERE'S AN UNIDENTIFIED **PRINT** ON THE NOTE — RIGHT THUMB. DOESN'T BELONG TO THE VICTIM. WE'RE RUNNING IT THROUGH RECORDS. JUST A CHANCE IT COULD BE OUR MANIAC.

YES... LEAVING HIS CALLING CARD.

NO POINT BREAKING THE RECORD IF YOU NEVER GET THE CREDIT.

THIS IS NUMBER ONE

WE'VE GOT I.D. ON SEVERAL OF THE VICTIMS. YOU WANT A RUNDOWN?

FORGET IT. A FEW SEVERED LIMBS AREN'T AREN'T GOING TO TELL ME ANYTHING. I'M GOING STRAIGHT TO THE EXPERT.

CONTROL — TELL **PSYCHO BLOCK 14** I'M ON MY WAY. SET UP AN INTERVIEW WITH **LEFTY**.

CONTINUED ON PAGE 41.

Anderson PSI DIVISION

REAL NAMES:	Cassandra Anderson
RANK/SOCIAL CATEGORY:	Judge, Psi Division
BASE OF OPERATIONS:	Mega-City One
TIME PERIOD:	2114 AD, Earth
GROUP AFFLIATIONS:	Psi Division, Justice Department, Mega-City One
FIRST APPEARANCE:	2000 AD Prog 150 "Judge Death" Part Two (February 1980)
CHARACTER HISTORY	After a troubled childhood Cassandra Anderson was enrolled as a cadet judge where her psi powers manifested themselves. After graduating she soon became one of the best psi judges with a reputation for irreverence and eccentricity. Despite these factors (forbidden amongst ordinary judges), she is one of Mega-City One's finest and has been Judge Dredd's ally in defeating major menaces like the Dark Judges, the Mutant and the Sisters of Death.

Anderson PSI DIVISION
GEORGE

Writers:	ALAN GRANT
Artist:	RUSSELL FOX
Lettering:	ELLIE DE VILLE
Status:	Just an average, ordinary day for Anderson as she investigates the case of George, the gigantic satanic tapeworm!

SO WHAT WOULD *YOU* DO IF YOU HAD A GIGANTIC SATANIC TAPEWORM CALLED GEORGE LIVING INSIDE YOU?

RIGHT— *I* WENT TO *THE DOC*, TOO. AND WHAT DOES *HE* DO?

EXAMINE ME? NO. REFER ME TO A SPECIALIST? NO.

OHMYGRUD! WH-WHAT ARE YOU GOING TO *DO*...?

I'D HAVE THOUGHT THAT'S *OBVIOUS!*

BUT I WANT YOU TO KNOW— IT'S NOT *MY* FAULT. THERE'S A *GIANT SATANIC TAPEWORM* CALLED *GEORGE* LIVING INSIDE ME. HE *MAKES* ME *KILL* FOLKS!

THE DOC JUST LOOKED AT ME THROUGH THOSE THICK PEBBLE GLASSES, AND SAID--

Y-Y-YOU'RE *CRAZY!*

I KILLED THE DO... AS WELL. GEORG... THOUGHT IT BEST...

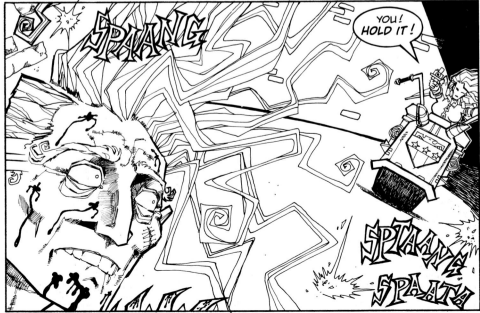

THE

Red Razors

REAL NAMES:	"Razors"
RANK/SOCIAL CATEGORY:	Judge
BASE OF OPERATIONS:	Sov-Block Two
TIME PERIOD:	2177 AD, Earth
GROUP AFFLIATIONS:	Sov-Block Two Judges
FIRST APPEARANCE:	Judge Dredd The Megazine (Volume 1) 8, "Red Razors" (May 1991)
CHARACTER HISTORY	Judge Razors was originally a member of Sov-Block Two's most notorious street gang, the Red Deths. He was eventually captured, tried and condemned to death. But instead of being executed he was instead used as a scientific guinea pig for experimentation. Doctors performed neuro-surgery on his brain to try and cancel his anti-social tendencies, harnessing his violent streak to work for the State. The operation has proved successful so far, with Razors' most famous case involving outwitting the mutant judges of Sov-Block One and recovered the holy corpse of Elvis Presley. But there always remains the danger he could begin reverting to his old ways...

Red Razors
Doctor's Orders

Writers:	MARK MILLAR
Artist:	STEVE YEOWELL
Lettering:	ANNIE PARKHOUSE
Status:	A sinister street gang stalks the citizens of Sov-Block Two, performing unnecessary operations - beware the Psycho Surgeons!

SOV BLOCK 2.

ARE YOU *SURE* I WON'T NEED AN ANAESTHETIC, DOCTOR?

WE'RE *MEDICAL* MEN, MISTER KINSKI. PROFESSIONALS IN EVERY SENSE. WE KNOW *EXACTLY* WHAT WE'RE DOING.

IT'S JUST THAT I'VE NEVER BEEN IN HOSPITAL BEFORE.

I DIDN'T KNOW YOU HAD TO BE STRAPPED INTO A *STEEL FRAME* BEFORE AN OPERATION.

STANDARD PROCEDURE, MISTER KINSKI.

NOW LIE STILL AND WE'LL GET THIS OVER WITH.

BUT ARE YOU *SURE* IT WON'T HURT? I MEAN, I ALWAYS THOUGHT HAVING MY APPENDIX REMOVED WOULD BE REALLY *PAINFUL.*

ANY WORD ON THE PSYCHO SURGEONS, RAZORS?

CAME UP ZIP, CONTROL. WASTED HALF AN HOUR ASKING QUESTIONS AT THE TAMMY WYNETTE COUNTRY AND WESTERN SALOON...

STILL, KEEPS ME IN SHAPE.

MICHAELA KENOBI, WACADAY NEWS. ANY TRUT TO THE RUMOUR THAT THIS ANOTHER PSYCHO SURGEON MURDER, JUDGE?

NO COMMENT. WE HAVEN'T EXAMINED THE BODY PROPERLY YET.

THIS MAY EVE HAVE BEE ACCIDEN DEATH.

COME ON, JUDGE—NOBODY GAROTTES THEMSELVES WITH A LAS-SAW!

YOU WANNA WALK WITH CRUTCHES, COMRADE? OUT OF MY DROKKIN' WAY!

SURGEONS LEAVE US ANOTHER STIFF, THEN, HANKERSON?

YEAH. THIS POOR JERK BRINGS THE DEATH-TOLL TO OV THIRTY, RAZORS.

GEEZ. DOESN'T PAY TO LOOK A LITTLE UNDER THE WEATHER WITH THOSE CREEPS RUNNING AROUND, HUH?

I SPENT THE REST OF THE NIGHT PATROLLING THE STREETS, LOOKING FOR THE PSYCHO SURGEONS IN THE SEEDIEST AREAS.

HARD TO BELIEVE THEY WERE ALL RESPECTED DOCTORS NOT SO LONG AGO.

THEIR ATTACKS ARE BECOMING MORE AND MORE FREQUENT AND ALL UNITS ARE ON FULL ALERT.

JUDGE! JUDGE RAZORS!

OVER HERE, MAN. THIS OLE LADY NEEDS SOME HELP!

WHAT'S THE PROBLEM, GRAN?

THAT CREEP JUST MADE OFF WITH HER PURSE.

CRIPPLE THE PERP, BOY! BREAK SUMTHIN' FER ME!

WE'D BEEN COMBING EVERY CORNER OF THE CITY FOR DAYS. PETTY CROOKS COULDN'T SPIT ON THE SIDEWALK WITHOUT A JUDGE BOOKING THEM.

BEEP BEEP

HOW COULD ANYONE DO THAT TO AN OLD WOMAN IN AN EXO-SKELETON — THESE CREEPS MAKE ME SICK, ED.

I DUNNO, RAZORS.

FRANKLY, I THINK THE GUY SHOWS SOME INITIATIVE!

COME ON, MEATHEAD.

I'LL MAKE THIS HURT A WHOLE LOT LESS IF YOU GIVE YOURSELF UP!

HE'S WAKING UP.

CAN WE KILL HIM NOW, HUH? CAN WE? HUH?

YOU'VE BEEN A NAUGHTY JUDGE, HAVEN'T YOU, RAZORS? YOU'VE CAUSED US A WHOLE LOT OF TROUBLE.

AND WE DON'T LIKE THAT, DO WE, BOYS?

THAT'S WHY WE'RE GIVING YOU THE *FULL AUTOPSY TREATMENT!*

WHO THE HELL ARE YOU?

I'M *THE CONSULTANT.* HEAD OF THE DEPARTMENT. CHIEF SURGEON.

I SAW THE LIGHT AND EMBRACED THE DARKNESS. IT'S MY MISSION TO END THE SUFFERING AND THE PAIN OF MANKIND.

THEY USED TO MAKE US WORK A TWENTY HOUR DAY, CAN YOU BELIEVE THAT?

THEN THEY TRIED TO STRETCH THE FABRIC OF REALITY. THEY TRIED TO MAKE US WORK A *TWENTY FIVE* HOUR DAY.

CAN'T YOU UNDERSTAND WHAT THAT DID TO OUR *HEADS?*

IT'S GONNA BE *NUTHIN'* COMPARED TO WHAT I'M GONNA DO TO YOU, *SLIME-BALL.*

YOU'RE GOING TO *DIE* HERE, JUDGE RAZORS.

NOBODY'S GOING TO SAVE YOU. NOBODY EVEN KNOWS WHERE YOU ARE.

YOU'RE GOING TO DIE ON THAT TABLE. TONIGHT. NOW.

THE E

JUDGE DREDD IN ATLANTIS

PART ONE

Script — J. WAGNER
Art — B. McCARTHY
Lettering — T. FRAME

A MILE BENEATH THE **BLACK ATLANTIC,** MIDWAY BETWEEN **MEGA-CITY ONE** AND **BRIT-CIT,** LIES THE MASSIVE UNDERSEA **CITY** OF **ATLANTIS** —

THE LARGEST OF SIX **SERVICE COMPLEXES** ALONG THE ROUTE OF THE **ATLANTIC TUNNEL, ATLANTIS** HAS BECOME A TOURIST ATTRACTION IN ITS OWN RIGHT...

DESPITE THE GREAT **DEPTH** AND THE HIGH DEGREE OF **POLLUTION,** LADIES AND GENTS, MANY MARINE LIFEFORMS — BOTH **MUTATED** AND **NORMAL** — THRIVE HERE.

FROM THE **SPINY NEON TURBOT** TO THE **DUCK-BILLED RAKFISH**...

CENTRE-DOME WE HAVE A **POISONOUS SPIDER STAR**.

BUT THE **REAL** STARS OF OUR SHOW ARE NOT HERE YET. SOME **MEAT SUBSTITUTE** IS NOW BEING RELEASED TO ATTRACT THEM.

CAN YOU SEE IT!

THAT **GLOWING** - COMING THIS WAY!

AND HERE THEY ARE!

OVER **100 FEET** FROM LANTERN TIP TO TAIL - COVERED IN LIVING, GROWING **CORAL**.

THE **CORAL RAY'S** JAWS ARE CAPABLE OF BITING THROUGH **TWO INCH REINFORCED STEEL**.

HEY, LOOK! AMONG THE MEAT SUBSTITUTE...

IT-IT'S A **HUMAN BODY!**

SKREEEEEEE

JUDGE POST ON **ATLANTIS** IS **JOINTLY** RUN BY FORCES OF **MEGA-CITY ONE** AND **BRIT-CIT** —

THERE'S NO NEED FOR THIS! I'M AN EXPERIENCED DRIVER! I CAN WEAVE!

NOT FOR THE NEXT TWELVE MONTHS YOU CAN'T!

YOU'RE WANTED OVER AT THE **SHOWDOME**, DREDD. SEEMS SOME JOKER GOT HIMSELF MIXED UP IN THE **CORAL RAYS'** LUNCH. LONSDALE'S ALREADY THERE.

DD PARKS...

...HE WHAT... ...JAWS...

SHOWDOME

ELECTRO-CANNON READY...

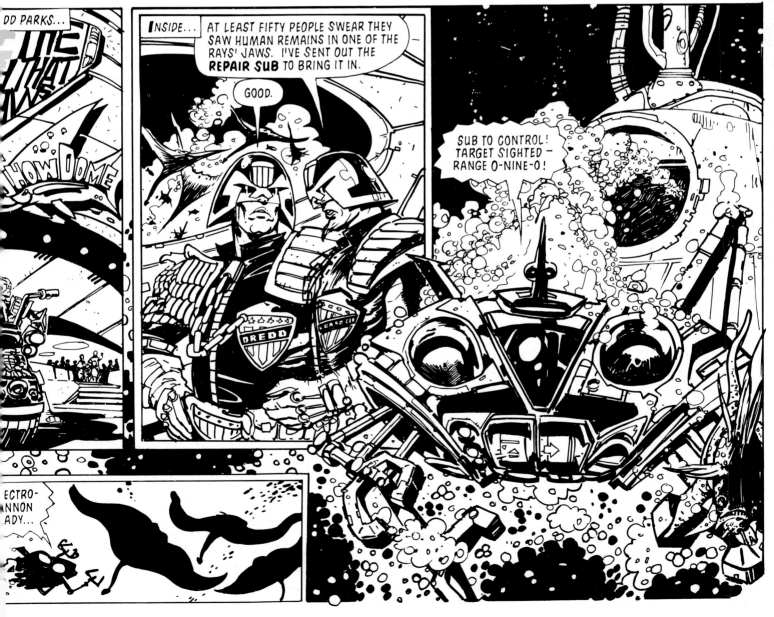

INSIDE... AT LEAST FIFTY PEOPLE SWEAR THEY SAW HUMAN REMAINS IN ONE OF THE RAYS' JAWS. I'VE SENT OUT THE **REPAIR SUB** TO BRING IT IN.

GOOD.

SUB TO CONTROL! TARGET SIGHTED — RANGE 0-NINE-0!

THERE'S YOUR ANSWER, DREDD...

DEFINITELY HUMAN!

IT HAD BEEN NINE YEARS SINCE THEY'D BEEN OFF **ATLANTIS**... SINCE, IN FACT, **LESLIE** WAS BORN. OH, **ERIC** HAD BEEN UP TO THE **BIG MEG** A COUPLE OF TIMES FOR HIS EX-BLOCK REUNIONS – AND SHE TRIED TO GET TO **BRIT-CIT** AT LEAST **ONCE** A YEAR...

BUT THEY'D NEVER BEEN AWAY TOGETHER. NOT FOR NINE YEARS.

CHATTING TO THE TOURISTS, FINDING OUT ALL ABOUT THEM...

NOT THAT SHE MINDED, REALLY. SHE WAS HAPPY ENOUGH HERE IN **ATLANTIS**, GOING ABOUT HER DAILY ROUTINE IN THE **CAPTAIN NEMO SOYFISH BAR**...

CAPTAIN NEMO SOYFISH BAR

SOMETIMES EVEN INVITING THEM BACK TO HER HOME AND MURDERING THEM.

YOU'RE **ELOPING**! HOW ROMANTIC!

WE'LL PHONE OUR FOLKS WHEN WE GET TO **BRIT-CIT**. THEN THERE'LL BE NOTHING THEY CAN DO TO STOP US!

SO YOU HAVEN'T TOLD A SOUL? VERY WISE!

SHE ALWAYS PHONED **ERIC** BEFORE BRINGING "GUESTS" HOME –

WHAT?

I SAID, THE **JUDGES** HAVE FOUND **BRIAN**.

B-BUT HOW?

I DON'T KNOW. THE **RAYS** USUALLY TAKE THE BODIES AS SOON AS I PUT THEM OUT OF THE **WETLOCK**. HIS MUST HAVE BEEN CAUGHT BY A FREAK CURRENT.

ANYWAY, THE AUDIENCE AT THE **SHOWDOME** GOT A RINGSIDE VIEW AND OLD **BRIAN** WAS THE MAIN COURSE.

OH MY GRUD! WHAT ARE WE GOING TO DO?

DON'T PANIC! NOBODY CAN TIE ANYTHING TO US, AUDREY. WE JUST CARRY ON AS NORMAL.

WE CAN'T!

WE'VE GOT TO! DOC DUCKWORTH'S **PAYMENT'S** DUE. BRIAN STILL LEFT US A **THOUSAND** SHORT.

HE CHECKED EVERY DETAIL WITH HER CAREFULLY. HAD SHE FOUND SOMEONE? YES, A YOUNG COUPLE. NO ONE KNEW THEY WERE HERE. THEY'D COME ON THE BUS, SO THERE WAS NO CAR TO DISPOSE OF. THAT WAS IMPORTANT.

CASH?

SHE'D SEEN HIS WALLET. IT WAS BULGING.

I'LL GET EVERY-THING READY. PULL YOURSELF TOGETHER. GET ON WITH IT.

YOU LOVEBIRDS! I'VE BEEN TELLING MY HUSBAND **ALL** ABOUT YOU!

THEIR NAMES WERE **JOHN** AND **MARY**. SUCH A NICE YOUNG COUPLE. SO MUCH IN LOVE.

KLIKK!

IT WAS EASY TO LURE THEM BACK TO THE APARTMENT: HER SHIFT ENDED IN HALF AN HOUR— ERIC HAD A BOTTLE OF SHAMPAIGN ALL READY— THEY SIMPLY **MUST** COME!

AH! OUR ROMEO AND JULIET! COME IN, COME IN!

SHE WOULD HAVE PREFERRED IT, OF COURSE, IF *LESLIE* HADN'T BEEN THERE. IT COULDN'T BE GOOD FOR THE BOY.

BETTER GET THE TOWELS, MUM. SHE'S *FROTHIN'*!

ERIC WAS VERY GOOD WITH THEM. SO KIND AND PATIENT...

WHY... WHY?

NOTHING PERSONAL, JOHN. IT'S OUR DOCTOR. HE'S BLACKMAILING US.

LESLIE REALLY *IS* A MUTANT, YOU SEE. FOR NINE YEARS WE'VE KEPT HIM HIDDEN HERE. IF WE DON'T MAKE OUR MONTHLY PAYMENT, OLD DUCKWORTH WILL TELL THE JUDGES.

ANYWAY, SORRY IF THAT'S HURTING A BIT. ONLY POISON I COULD GET HOLD OF.

TRY TO RELAX— GO WITH IT. IT'LL BE OVER SOON.

MUST BE SIXTEEN HUNDRED CREDS CASH HERE. WAY TO PICK 'EM, HON!

JUDGE DREDD IN ATLANTIS

CONCLUDES ON PAGE 62

DEMOCRACY!

What the papers said...

THE CRY FOR DEMOCRACY MUST BE HEARD!

THE TIME has come to stand against the tyranny of the Judges.

It is time to remove power from our self-elected overlords and return it to where it belongs - in the hands of the people!

The Judges would have us believe that there is no alternative to the dictatorial and often brutal form of government. The Democratic Tendency has an historic responsibility to nail this lie and we will not rest until our message is heard. To this end we have launched our "Democratic charter" and we urge all free-thinking citizens to support our demands:

An immediate return to democratic principles. The people must control the Judges! The Judges should not control the people!

The return of basic freedoms taken away over decades of oppression!

A repeal of the harsh penalties for minor infringements!

Publicising our new charter will be no easy task, as the Judges fear democracy, knowing that it will result in them losing power. We know that our demands will find many echoes throughout Mega-City One and we are prepared to go to almost any length to make our voice heard.

The Times of Mega-City, March 13, 2108

STOP PRESS

Reports that this morning's breakfast show on Channel 48 was briefly interrupted by a terrorist attack have been confirmed by the Justice Department. Due to the Judges' rapid response to the situation there were no civilian casualities, but the terrorists, who were all heavily-armed, were killed when the Judges returned their fire.

YOU IN THERE! RELEASE THE HOSTAGES AND SURRENDER OR WE COME IN SHOOTING!

MURDERED

MARCH 13, 2108, is a date that will live in infamy in the history of Mega-City One.

Four members of the Democratic Tendency whose only "crime" was to stand up for the principles of freedom and democracy were brutally slain by the Judges.

The names of Hester Hyman, Franklin Lund, J. William Williams and Roofer Tuttle will always be remembered as martyrs of the democratic movement.

Their valiant attempt to seize control Channel 48 was doomed to failure, b not before Hester was able announce our "Democratic Charter" li on air. Then, despte offering resistance, she and the three oth freedom fighters were gunned down the Judges stormed the station.

The citizens of Mega-City One will r stand for this kind of treatment. T Democratic Tendency will go fro strength to strength as a result of t act of murder by the Judges.

Millet Street Parish News, March 14, 2108

THOUGHT FOR THE DAY

Bishop Desmond Snodgrass writes...

Have you ever had a day that turned out quite differently to the way you expected it would? The big guy up there likes to throw the odd wobbler at us like that, you know. It keeps you on your toes, so to speak. I certainly had a day like that yesterday!

I got up early to appear on Channel 48's breakfast show to explain why out church opposes the wearing of knee-pads by the clergy and before I knew it I was mistaken for one of those pop star fellows! Now, while it was quite flattering to be confused with one of Mega-City

One's best-loved - ahem! - "sex symbols", I was taken aback to say the least. Then, if you will pardon the expression, all hell broke loose!

Some of those democrat chappies broke in and took over the studio. Bullets were flying all over the place I can tell you, especially when the Judges arrived to sort them out. The whole experience taught me something, though - it doesn't matter how hard you try to avoid them, sex and violence always seem to rear their ugly heads and I really think it is about time something was done about it.

Democratic Bulletin, July 24, 2108

TIME TO MARCH!

by Blondel Dupre

ON MARCH 13, 2108, Hester Hyman, Franklin Lund, J. William Williams and Roofer Tuttle were shot down in cold blood by the forces of so-called law and order.

They had hurt no one, they offered no resistance. They accepted their fate in the knowledge that each death, each sacrifice is a step in the direction of freedom. The Democratic Tendency are only the best documented example of decent, ordinary citizens willing to die for a cause they believe to be just - the return of power to the hands of the people!

Since the Sons of the Constitution, the Freedom League, the Democratic Urge and the Committee for the Restoration of civil Liberties came together under the banner of the Hester Hyman Trust, the cry for democracy has grown even louder. Now we have formed the Democratic Charter Group to provide a focus for our demands.

Next week we will march on the Hall of Justice to present the Judges with our demands as embodied in the Charter of the Democratic Tendency. There will be no violence. We will give them no excuse to beat us down with their guns and their daysticks. We will march not with the clenched fist of anger, but with the open palm of peace. Yet our demands will sound no less loudly - power to the people!

Democrat, March 21, 2108

OBITUARY: HESTER HYMAN

HESTER HYMAN was murdered by the Judges during the heroic takeover of Channel 48 by the Democratic Tendency last week. She leaves a husband, Gort, and two sons, Simson and Gort Junior.

Hester was just an ordinary citizen who wanted a decent future for her children. She could see them growing up as frightened people, only fit for taking orders from the self-appointed overlords, the Judges. Hester saw her children's future and it terrified her. Because she loved them, she chose to sacrifice her life to change it.

When a good mother must act to change the society her children grow up in, then something is badly wrong with that society. Hester Hyman died a martyr's death and in doing so she has become more than a person, she has become a symbol for the whole democratic movement.

The Democratic Tendency has therefore set up the Hester Hyman Trust, in the hope that all of the rival democratic factions can by united under its banner. The best way to honour her memory will be for all democrats to join together and ensure that the Judges' days are numbered. Together we will have democracy!

The Times of Mega-City, July 29, 2109

DEMOCRACY...HMMPH!

CHIEF JUDGE SILVER dismissed democracy as an old chestnut yesterday.

"There's always some lunatic group dragging it out of the fire," he told media correspondents. "We tried democracy before and it doesn't work."

Silver insisted that the Judges are the peoples' best friends, far from being their enemy, as the democrats suggest.

"If we keep a tight grip on the people, it is for their own good," explained the Chief Judge.

"Without us, the city would collapse into chaos and anarchy. It has happened before and I have no intention of allowing it to happen again."

However, he went on to say that he would not be banning the march planned by the Democratic Charter Group.

"We are not tyrants. We will never seek to deny our citizens the right of peacefuol demonstration," pledged Silver.

As long as the marchers remain within the law, it is clear that the Judges will tolerate their actions.

News of the Meg, July 30, 2109

DIRTY DEM DAME!

BARMY BETHANN Rosie, loony leader of the radical Civil Liberties committee, has being taking a few liberties herself!

The wanton woman was arrested this morning on four - **count 'em, four!** - counts of bigamy.

Her mega-marriage mayhem could grab the *un-bridled* Bethann a wedding bouquet of up to 20 years in the cubes - what a honeymoon!

All four of her unfortunate "husbands" slammed the **scarlet antics** of Rosie, one of the leaders of today's dangerous democratic demo.

"You have to wonder what someone of Bethann's *low moral standards* is doing leading any kind of march," said one and we are forced to agree.

The News of the Meg believes personalities should not influence Mega-City politics, but anyone who follows **dirty dem** leader Bethann Rosie on the march must be as *morally bankrupt* as her!

The Times of Mega-City, July 30, 2109

DEMOCRAT LEADER IN SOV SCANDAL

MAJOR EVIDENCE of Sov infiltration of the Democratic Charter Group was found last night.

Morton Phillipps, chairman of the Freedom League and a leader in today's march for Democracy, was revealed as a collaborator with Sov forces during the Apocalypse War.

Several witnesses came forward to talk of Phillipps' wartime activities, including one r who had been sentencec death by the democrats' lea A photograph of Phillipp full Sov uniform has also b uncovered by our reporters.

The revelations have bro howls of protest from popular media, deman Phillipps to answer for his crimes. A question mark hangs over his leadershi today's democrat march.

STOP PRESS!

KENZAL DAVITCHEK may be unable to lead the Sons of the Constitution in the democratic march today.

The veteran freedom campaigner was kept on his feet all last night while held on trumped-up charges by the charges.

This was obviously an attempt to make him drop out of today's march but Kenzal has promised to do his best to lead us to the steps of the so-called "Hall of Justice".

Gort Hyman, with his sons Simson and Gort Junior, yesterday

DON'T GO ON THIS MARCH OF INSANITY!

The Times of Mega-City, July 31, 2109

VIOLENCE ERUPTS ON DEMOCRATIC MARCH

FRUSTRATION at the poor turnout on the democratic march yesterday led to a massive outbreak of violence by the "peaceful" demonstrators.

The Judges were forced to intervene to prevent a bloodbath and several thousand protestors were arrested for violent and disorderly conduct.

Chief Judge Silver last night conceded he had been wrong not banning the march.

"If the disgusting incidents we witnessed yesterday are an example of democracy at work, then I trust everyone of you has learned a valuable lesson," he said in a live broadcast to the city.

"Freedom is a fine ideal, but too much freedom is a dangerous thing.

"Yes, our laws are harsh. Yes, our freedoms are subject to certain restrictions. Not because we want it to be this way, but because it must be this way."

"If it had not been for the prompt action of my judges, there is no telling what devastation would have be brought upon this city - all in the name of democracy!"

THE LEADER of today's democratic march has admitted he was wrong!

Gort Hyman, widower of the democrat "martyr" Hester Hyman (below), is begging citizens not to join the dirty dem march.

He told us exclusively last night that his wife was misguided in her beliefs:

"If only Hester could have seen the chaos she was wishing on us all. Without the Judges this city would become a jungle, a nightmare!"

Democratic Bulletin, July 31, 2109

JUDGES CRUSH MARCH!

SIXTEEN MILLION people joined the march for democracy yesterday before it was illegally crushed by the so-called forces of Law.

Despite the Judges' efforts to sabotage it, yesterday's march was the largest expression of anger over their misrule since the Judges seized power for themselves nearly 40 years ago.

Many thousands of marchers were killed or injured. Among those arrested were Blondel Dupre, the only one of our leaders the Judges allowed to take part.

Before they threw her in the cubes she had the following warning for the judges:

"You can beat us with your boots and your daysticks, but you can't crush our ideals!

"Freedom, truth, democracy - they all live where you can't touch them, in the hearts of the people.

"And one day they're going to beat you!"

The Times of Mega-City, March 8, 2112

MERCY ON DEMOCRATS

THE JUSTICE DEPARTMENT announced yesterday that 63 people arrested after the march for democracy turned into a riot three years ago are to be released.

Among those to be released is Blondel Dupre, leader of the Democratic Urge group and leader of the march.

No reason has been given for the release of the prisoners, some of whom still have up to 27 years to serve.

Sources close to the Hall of Justice suggest that Judge Dredd himself signed the release papers, which would signal a major change in attitude by the veteran.

Democratic activists were stunned and sceptical at the announcement yesterday.

"I'll believe it when I see it," said one.

Democratic Bulletin, November 1, 2112

JUDGES OUT!

IF EVER the Judges had any credible claim to rule o city, it was linked to their ability to protect t citizens.

When they allowed Judge Death to take over Meg City One and turn it into a Necropolis, they gave this claim.

How can anyone ever trust them again, when many of the Judges actually aided the Dark Judg rather than opposed them?

The time has come for the people to take pow before the Judges have time to reimpose their unj rule upon us.

Let us make just one demand of them - we dem democracy and we demand it now!

PEOPLE'S POLL ANNOUNCED!

"LET THE PEOPLE DECIDE!"

That was the *shock stunner* from Judge Dredd today.

The Big Meg's greatest Judge left others **speechless** as he announced a referendum about who should run MC-1.

"Firm control, rigid discipline, instant justice. That's what I stand for and I'm willing to put it to *the people!*" he said.

News of the Meg can only agree with this - the Dark Judges killed 60 million citizens during Necropolis and the Judges helped!

How can we ever trust them again? Only the people can decide if the Judges still have *the right* to govern!

Some Judges oppose the poll and the **dirty dems** are claiming the vote is a trick.

Their attitude is typical of trouble-makers who just want to destabilize the city, *even when getting what they've always wanted!*

We stand by this decision by Judge Dredd - he puts the people and justice first, just like the **News of the Meg!**

Democratic News, October 9, 2113

VOTE FOR DEMOCRACY!

NOVEMBER 1, 2113, will be an historic day as 40 years of oppression by the Judges is finally ended!

They face an overwhelming defeat in the referendum - the best they can do is promote scare stories about criminals running wild in a democratic society.

This ignores the face that there will be law enforcement under democracy. The different strands within the Democratic Coalition favour different methods of policing the city, but ultimate power must never again reside with these "police".

The Judges have taught us the folly of this form of government and now at last we have the opportunity of telling them this.

Millet St Parish News, October 16, 2113

VOTE WITH YOUR FEET

Bishop Desmond Snodgrass writes...

Amid this "referendum fever", it's easy to forget the important things in life.

No, not this issue thing about whether knee-pades can ever be compatible with religion. I've been into that many times.

I'm talking about coming down to the Church on Millet Street. Not nearly enough of you do, you know. Indeed, a few people have suggested that we should relocate the church to the public vid-phone box on the corner.

So I am asking you all to think hard when you cast your vote in the coming referendum and then to vote with your feet by coming to the Church.

I've even put up some rather nice wallpaper to brighten the place up a bit. It's lovely, it really is.

The Times of Mega-City, October 23, 2113

CONSPIRACY?

RUMOURS OF a conspiracy against Judge Dredd, and next week's referendum, were circulating widely last night.

The Justice Department would neither confirm nor deny reports from within the Halls of Justice that a secret cabal of senior Judges opposing the referendum attempted to assassinate Judge Dredd.

Apparently the conspiracy has been crushed but all details are being kept firmly under wraps by the Judges in the lead-up to the referendum next week.

A vocal opponent of the referendum, Judge Grice, was unavailable for comment.

The Times of Mega-City, November 2, 2113

Better the devil you know?

DEMOCRACY REJECTED was the overwhleming outcome of yesterday's historic referendum.

The Judges received a massive 68% of the votes in the poll, with another 23% declared invalid.

Only 9% voted in favour.

Analysts said the poll demonstrated the people's tendency towards the status quo - better the devil you know than the democrat you don't, one pundit said!

Judge Dredd instigated the referendum, the first in Mega-City One's history, and he summed the result up by saying:

"Democracy's not for the people - not because we say so, but because they don't want it."

Hundreds of thousands of democrats took to the streets after hearing the result, claiming the Judges had rigged the result.

Dredd denied foul play: "We didn't fix anything - we didn't have to!"

Just when a repeat of the street violence from the democrat's march of four years ago looked likely, Judge Dredd confronted Blondel Dupre.

Below: A citizen votes

REFERENCES

2000 AD progs

460:	"Letter from a Democrat"
531-533:	"Revolution" Parts 1-3
668:	"Tale of the Dead Man" Part 7
702-706:	"Nightmares" Parts 1-5
750-753:	"The Devil You Know" Parts 1-4
754-756:	"Twilight's Last Gleaming" Parts 1-3

A CRAZED **SERIAL KILLER** IS TONIGHT **TERRORISING** MEGA-CITY ONE!

THE KILLER, WHO IS ARMED WITH A HIGH-POWERED LASER **DISINTEGRATOR GUN**, HAS STRUCK **TWICE** SO FAR, KILLING **EIGHT** CITIZENS IN A SECTOR TWENTY FOUR 'DUST ZONE AND, LATER, A FURTHER **NINETEEN** PEOPLE DIED AT A 237TH STREET HOV STATION, BRINGING THE TOTAL DEAD TO **TWENTY SEVEN!**

11.04

AND — WAIT A MINUTE — I'M JUST GETTING WORD OF **MORE** KILLINGS!

YES! WE'RE TAKING YOU STRAIGHT OVER TO **DENNIS NELSON** AT THE SCENE—

11.04

THANK YOU, GLENDA!

I'M AT THE **BLOCKTOPS** ELDSTERS' REST HOME IN SECTOR 17, WHERE ONLY MINUTES AGO JUDGES MADE ANOTHER GRISLY DISCOVERY —

11.05

THE **KILLER** HAS **STRUCK AGAIN!** FIFTY NINE ELDSTERS ARE DEAD!

FIFTY NINE ELDSTERS — MANY OF THEM TOO WEAK AND FRAIL TO FLEE THEIR ATTACKER—MANY UNABLE TO **COMPREHEND** THE HORRIBLE BUT EXTREMELY NEWSWORTHY CARNAGE BEING WROUGHT AROUND THEM!

FIFTY NINE HELPLESS SENIOR CITIZENS, DISINTEGRATED WHERE THEY STOOD — BLOWN OUT OF EXISTENCE IN ONE EXCITINGLY MURDEROUS FRENZY!

AND ALL THAT IS LEFT OF THEM IS THEIR **SEVERED RIGHT ARMS**, FOR THIS IS THE KILLER'S DISTINCTIVE **TRADEMARK**.

SERIAL KILLER
PART **2**

HANDS ACROSS THE WATER

AND IF I HELP YOU...YOU'LL GET ME A **CUBE** WITH A **VIEW**?

THERE'S NO SUCH THING, BLATTY.

HOW ABOUT YOU **DON'T** HELP ME AND I GET YOU A COURSE OF 'LECTRO THERAPY?

YOU'RE A VERY PERSUASIVE MAN, DREDD.

ALL RIGHT... I'LL TELL YOU TWO THINGS.

THE FIRST IS... YOU'VE ALREADY **LOST** HIM.

I DID MY KILLINGS IN THREE HOURS. HE'LL WANT TO DO THE SAME OR BETTER.

IT'S ELEVEN TWENTY EIGHT— NEARLY TWO AND A HALF HOURS, IF HE STARTED AT NINE. THAT'S ENOUGH TIME. THAT WOULD BE HIS TARGET.

WHEN YOU CAUGHT ME YOU KNEW ABOUT LESS THAN **HALF** MY KILLINGS — I HAD TO TELL YOU ABOUT THE REST. THIS TIME YOU KNOW ABOUT — **NINETY FOUR**?

SO HOW MANY **HAVEN'T** YOU DISCOVERED?

NO, MY GUESS IS HE'S ALREADY **GOT** THE RECORD — HE'S ALREADY ON HIS WAY OUT OF THE CITY.

OUT OF THE CITY?

THAT'S THE SECOND THING. THE KILLER COMES FROM BRIT-CIT.

HOW DO I KNOW? BECAUSE HE'S AFTER **MY** RECORD! **MY** RECORD!

AND YOU WON'T FIND MY NAME IN **CASTLE'S MEGAREC**! OH NO, NOT ONE WORD! I'M NOT **RECOGNISED** IN MY **OWN** CITY! IT'S ONLY **NEWTON**! MAD TONY NEWTON! THAT WIMP!

BUT IN **BRIT-CIT**, NOW— THEY **KNOW** HOW TO RECOGNISE GENIUS!

SEE—HERE IN THE **BRIT-CIT BOOK** OF **RECORDS**--

BRIT-CIT! THEY KNOW ABOUT ME THERE! THAT'S WHERE THE COPYCAT COMES FROM!

SERIAL KILLINGS

MOST KILLINGS

THE GREATEST NUMBER OF ONE-ON-ONE MURDERS IN A SINGLE 24 HOUR PERIOD WERE COMMITTED BY ANTHONY 'MAD TONY' NEWTON OF MEGA-CITY ONE ON MARCH 14th 2102. IN THE SPACE OF 8 HOURS 194 VICTIMS BY THE UNUSUAL METHOD OF GAS INHALATION.

FASTEST:
BUT FOR SHEER SPEED, THE RECORD MUST GO TO JEAN PAUL BLATTY, ANOTHER RESIDENT OF MEGA-CITY ONE.
IN THE SPACE OF THREE SHORT HOURS ON JULY 7, 2105, BLATTY —NICKNAMED "LEFTY" — MURDERED 129 CITIZENS WITH A HEAVY-DUTY DISINTEGRATOR, LEAVING ONLY THEIR LEFT HANDS AS EVIDENCE OF THE CRIMES.
THIS WORKS OUT AT A KILLING AND DISINTERGRATION EVERY 83 SECONDS, A PHENOMENAL RECORD, AND MUST RANK BLATTY AS ONE OF THE TRULY GREATEST MURDERERS THE WORLD WILL EVER KNOW.

BUT **YOU'LL** NEVER FIND HIM! HA HA! BECAUSE I'VE LURED YOU WITHIN ARM'S REACH! AND NOW I'M GOING TO ADD YOU TO **MY** SCORE!

DON'T BE ABSURD.

NO WONDER YOU'RE IN A **PSYCHO** CUBE, BLATTY.

KLUNNNGG!

CONTROL—WE GOT A **MAKE** ON THAT THUMBPRINT FROM THE NOTE YET?

NEGATIVE.

JUST A CHANCE BLATTY COULD BE ON THE RIGHT TRACK. CHECK IT WITH **BRIT-CIT** RECORDS OFFICE.

THAT MAY NOT BE NECESSARY. GO TO GRUNDER PEDWAY— MAN AMOK WITH DISINTEGRATOR!

MASSAGE AND SAUNA

--HERE OUTSIDE **EXOTICA MASSAGE AND SAUNA**, WHERE THE **RIGHT ARM KILLER** HAS STRUCK AGAIN!

ARMS—RIGHT ARMS—CLIENT AND MASSEUSE, SILENTLY FLOATING—COMING TOGETHER AND PARTING, TUMBLING ENDLESSLY IN THIS GRIM BALLET OF DEATH—THIS LAST, GROTESQUE TANGO...

IN ALL, FOUR CUSTOMERS AND FIVE MEMBERS OF STAFF ARE DEAD. THIS BRINGS THE KILLER'S TALLY TO **ONE HUNDRED AND THREE**.

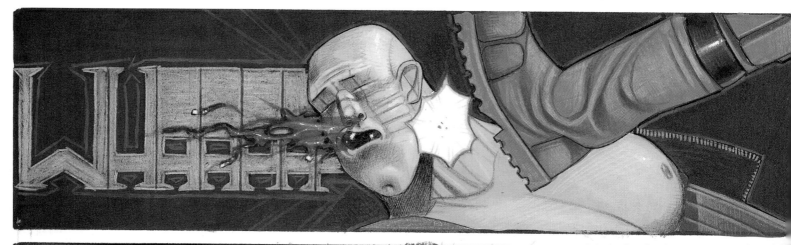

CONCLUDES ON PAG

Soul Sisters

REAL NAMES:	Sisters Susan Hope and Jocasta Faith
RANK/SOCIAL CATEGORY:	Vigilante nuns
BASE OF OPERATIONS:	Brit-Cit
TIME PERIOD:	2176 AD, Earth
GROUP AFFLIATIONS:	Former members of Little Sisters of Grud, branch of Global Church of Grud
FIRST APPEARANCE:	Judge Dredd The Megazine (Volume 2) 2, "The Soul Sisters" (May 1992)
CHARACTER HISTORY	The Soul Sisters are devoted followers of Grud and joined the Order of the Little Sisters of Grud to devote their lives to his work. However they rapidly became dismayed by the rampant commercialism within the convent and its inhabitants and decided to go it alone. Leaving just a curt note - "Drok this for a game of Christian Soldiers" - they escaped and launched themselves on a campaign to clean up the crime-infested streets of Brit-Cit. Operating from their Soul Sanctuary in the ruins of the abandoned Temple tube station, they have become the Scourge of the Street-Scum. Vigilantes with a vengeance, nuns with attitude - they are the Soul Sisters!

Soul Sisters
The Dark Nuns Return

Writers:	DAVID BISHOP & DAVE STONE
Artist:	SHAKY KANE
Lettering:	ELLIE DE VILLE
Status:	A hoax! A dream! An imaginery story! The Soul Sisters are dead and Brit-Cit has really gone to hell since their demise!

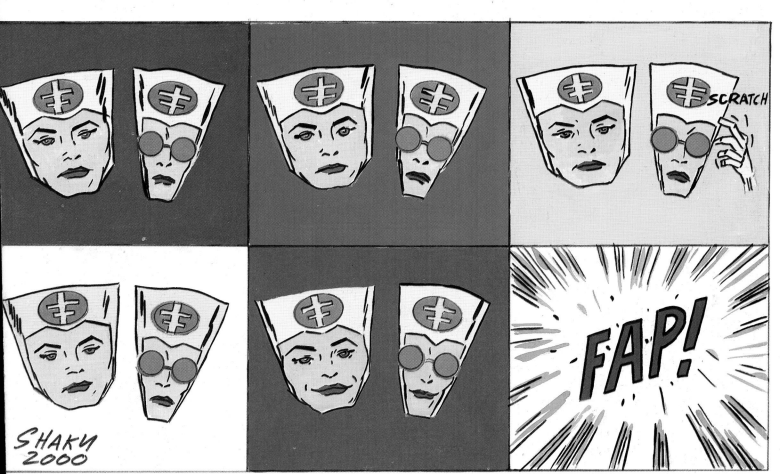

ARMITAGE

REAL NAME:	Armitage, first name unknown
RANK/SOCIAL CATEGORY:	Detective Judge
BASE OF OPERATIONS:	Brit-Cit
TIME PERIOD:	2114 AD, Earth
GROUP AFFLIATIONS:	Plainclothes Division, Justice Department, Brit-Cit
FIRST APPEARANCE:	
CHARACTER HISTORY:	Judge Dredd The Megazine (Volume 1) 9, "Armitage" (June 1991)

Very little is known about Detective Judge Armitage's background. He has extensive knowledge of the weapons used in the Brit-Cit Civil War of 2092-9. He considers himself a 'working judge', (as opposed to senior judges, who buy their commissions) and suffers fools and incompetents badly. Armitage is physically strong and quick but prefers to use brain over brawn. Pathologist Mary Turner has said of Armitage: "He's arrogant and abrasive and everybody hates him - but he's also the best detective judge in the city."

ARMITAGE
The Case Of The
Detonating
Dowager

Writer:	DAVE STONE
Illustrator:	SEAN PHILLIPS
Status:	Armitage and Rookie Judge Treasure Steel are returning to Brit-Cit by airship when something strange happens to the Dowager Duchess of Ghent.

With Apologies to
Aubrey Beardsley

A cold winter's night. Multi-coloured constellations pinwheeling overhead. The roar of the choppy, stroppy sea below, half-lost in the hum of Meuller-Fokker props. The flutter of canvas and the creak of hawsers.

Detective Judge Armitage and Rookie Judge Treasure Steel leant against the rail of the gondola catwalk, depressed.

They had tracked one Cornelius Pennyfeather - perpetrator of the fiendish Brit-Cit Electrified Bicycle Pump Murders - down in Euro-Cit, had cornered him...but the whole sorry affair had ended with Pennyfeather plunging from the mile-high extruded polymer replica of the Eiffel Tower into a vat of steaming *bouillabaisse*.

Such a *debacle*, Treasure reflected, could not leave anything other than a bad taste in the mouth. The resulting soup had been appalling, and tasted slightly of pork.

There had been nothing for it but to return to Brit-Cit by the most immediate available route - in this case, the Euro/Brit-Cit airship.

They had lived to regret it. Behind them, from the gondola proper came what was either the sound of a red-hot poker being forcibly inserted into a macaw, or shrill, srieking laughter. They winced.

Airships were a mode of transport for the rich and the well-bred, and in the course of the journey Armitage and Steel had come to know and loathe every one of the other passengers.

"Parasites." Armitage spat into the cruel sea below.

"Chinless drokking wonders," said Treasure.

"Grud, I need a drink," said Armitage.

The walls of the airship's lounge crawled with gilt and velvet plush in a particularly bilious shade of maroon. If you listened hard enough through the Muzak, you could hear the bells pealing from the minarets of civilisations lost in the Axminister shag. Red filters over the lights gave those the light fell upon the aspect of having been filleted.

At the bar, Armitage drank the latest in a long line of beers and glowered blearily at the barman until he produced another. Beside him, Treasure added bitter lemon into a stiff gin and surveyed the other occupants of the lounge:-

Across the bar, the slumped, ragged figure of Mr Roger Awl, method actor and dipsomaniac of no small renown, was regaling the world in general with the events of one evening in October, when he was far from sober, and dragging home a load with manly pride. Treasure knew from bitter experience that a pig would come into it later.

Beyond him, Ms Lobelia Romp-Specimen, the medicated goitre heiress and radiant in a glazed bread mask (which she raised and lowered on a small silver hoist), was tucking into a plate of lethal canapes and proffering *bon mots* to her tuxedo'd paramour, Rupert Glome-Rotring.

(Before sampling the cultural joys of Euro-Cit, Treasure had been under the impression that a *bon mot* was a sort of boiled sweet. She had been vaguely disappointed to find that it was in face a small and rather slimy form of witless epigram.) Beyond this pair, the Viscount Jeremy Temporal-Lobe was dancing stripped to the waist in the company of several like-minded friends, with many happy whoops and the nascent tang of body oil. Beyond them...

Beyond them, at a candle-lit table, in the company of a gigolo who had fallen on hard times, taken the job out of desperation and was now counting the hours until he was paid off, the Dowager Duchess of Ghent dropped her glass and clutched at her throat.

She coughed. She retched. And then with a hiss of gas she began to *inflate*.

Without pause for thought Treasure finished off her gin and lemon, bought a packet of nuts, grabbed a semi-comatose Armitage by the lapel and dragged him under the nearest table.

The Dowager exploded with a *bang* - leaving no trace but for the visceral and digestive matter splattered over the entire lounge and its occupants, and several slightly scorched lace veils fluttering to the floor like dying bats.

After a time, or possibly two times, Armitage and Steel crawled from under the table. Still cradling his half-finished and miraculously unspilled beer, Armitage glared around at the shocked and slathered masses.

"Probably some sort of meso-electric element in the drink," he said. "It disrupted her internal cellular pressure and *whamo!* I think we should..."

Steel never knew exactly what Armitage thought because at that moment the door flew open and in burst a short, portly figure with a bald and glistening head, a perambulatory moustache and his mouth wrapped around a churchwarden. (That's a pipe.)

It was M. Andre Dupont no less, gourmand and world-famous Euro-Cit amateur sleuth *par excellence!*

"There has been a murder here!" he cried. "Murder most foul. The Dowager Duchess of Ghent lies dead and, since we are at this very moment over international waters, *I* will investiage!"
"Suit yourself," said Armitage.

It was later. The lounge had been cleared by burly attendants, Dupont and the suspects had retired to the late Dowager's cabin to further the investigation. The suspects were Mr Roger Awl, Ms Lobelia Romp-Specimen, Mr Rupert Glome-Rotring, the Viscount Jeremy Temporal-Lobe, Ron the gigolo, Treasure and Armitage.

"Why us?" Armitage said indignantly.

"Wasn't it *lunchtime* you were shouting how you'd see the lot of us dead and screaming in hell, if you could get away with it?" Lobelia asked sweetly.

"She has a point," said Treasure.

Armitage muttered something to himself and amused himself by surreptitiously rifling through the late Dowager's drawers while Dupont questioned the suspects...

"I *loved* her!" sobbed Lobelia Romp-Specimen. "She was like a mother to me. Even the time she brutally dismembered my pet rad-hamster Crippen with a surgical bone-saw didn't matter, because I really, really..."

The Viscount seemed flustered. "I barely knew the woman," he said. "We moved in completely different circles. What possible reason could I have for -"

Armitage, meanwhile, had unearthed a large leather-bound dossier from the Dowager's steam trunk. With photos. He examined the contents, snorted, and passed them to Treasure.

Treasure raised an eyebrow at the Viscount, who was now turning a little green. "I like the bit about the electrodes, the Wellington boots and the genetically engineered livestock," she said. "It that physcially possible?"

The interrogations wore on. It transpired that Rupert Glome-Rotring was also featured in the shameful dossier. When the details were revealed, Lobelia Romp-Specimen clapped a hand to her mouth and ran from the cabin. She returned later - pale, wan and covered in breadcrumbs. Even

Seen '91

Armitage had felt slightly queasy.
Dupont made a note of several details for later.

Roger Awl then treated them to a song, detailing how he discovered his new bride to be a multiple amputee to the tune of *Side by Side*.

Ron the gigolo revealed that he *had* in fact been plotting to murder the Dowager by way of a stiletto and a butt of malmsey - but had never had the chance to put his plan into effect.

Dupont then turned his attention to Armitage and Steel, who revealed themselves as Brit-Cit Judges.

"*Alors*," he exclaimed at last, mopping his brow with a croissant, "I have to admit I am - how you say? - one stump short of a wicket."

"Hm," said Armitage. Thoughtfully.

There was something nagging at the back of his beer-soaked mind, something to do with the *sequence* of the murder. He pulled another can from those he had managed to save from the Dowager-bedecked bar, and downed it.

He climbed to his feet and wandered the cabin, counting off points on his fingers: "I think we can agree that the late Dowager exploded. A sound like that would suggest one of the *gasbags* blowing out rather than anything else...

Furthermore, after she died, the Dowager was in no state to be identified by a casual observer. There might be teeth and fingers and suchlike scattered round, but -"

"I think I got her glass eye," the Viscount said helpfully, reaching for his trouser pocket.

"Spare me." Armitage wandered over to the Dowager's steam trunk and gazed down thoughtfully on the shameful dossier.

"There was one person," he mused, "who *knew* that murder had been committed, *knew* who the victim was - but wasn't on the scene at the time!"

"I admit it!" the great detective cried, prostrate before the startled suspects. "I admit it all! I would also like three thousand, seven hundred and fifty similar offences to be taken into account, including matricide, fratricide and cattle rustling.

"I have roamed the world for *years*, slaughtering wherever I go and palming it off on some innocent bystander. My greatest triumph was the decimation of *three* Brit-Cit hab-blocks and laying the blame on an itinerant electrified bicycle-pump salesman!

"But," he continued, leaping to his feet, "you'll never take me alive!"

With that Dupont streak for the door. The suspects tried to stop him but to no avail, for he had taken the precaution of purloining the Viscount's body oil and had liberally coated himself with it. He slipped through their grasp and vanished into the night.

Enraged, the suspects took off after him, leaving the cabin empty save for Armitage, Steel and the fading sounds of running feet.

Armitage opened another beer and pulled a fob watch from a pocket. He studied it in silence.

After a while Treasure became aware of distant voices approaching. She went to the cabin door and listened.

"All *right*," said a slightly desperate Dupont. "You *can* take me alive."

"What do you think?" asked a voice instantly recognisable at that of Rupert Glome-Rotring.

Several voices held a muted conference followed by a "Heave!" in unison, a descending and faint cry of "*Merde!*" and a splash.

Armitage put his watch away. "By my reckoning we're now in Brit-Cit airspace," he said.

"Let's go nick these drokkers for conspiracy to commit murder by drowning."

THE END

COPIES OF FINGERPRINTS TAKEN FROM THE BODY FOUND IN THE **CORAL RAY'S** GUT ARE FLASHED TO THE CENTRAL COMPUTERS IN **BRIT-CIT** AND **MEGA-CITY ONE**. WITHIN MINUTES THE *I.D.* IS MADE —

BRIAN ROWLEY, AGE 37. RESIDENT BRIT-CIT DISTRICT NW6.

REPORTED MISSING YESTERDAY. LAST SEEN BY A NEIGHBOUR LEAVING HIS APARTMENT.

AND SOMEHOW HE MANAGED TO END UP AS **FISH FOOD** FIFTEEN HUNDRED MILES AWAY...

OKAY, LET'S START INTERROGATING **SHOWDOME** STAFF.

COULD BE ROWLEY WAS **ALREADY** DEAD WHEN HE GOT HERE. THE **FISH MEAT** COMES PRE-PACKED FROM A BRIT-CIT SUPPLIER.

SOMETHING HERE, DREDD — AN ARTIFICIAL HIP!

ROWLEY'S?

NOT UNLESS HE HAD THREE LEGS.

SO BRIAN ROWLEY'S NOT THE FIRST BODY TO END UP ON THE MENU.

INTERESTING...

REDD'S INTERROGATION OF THE STAFF OF THE SHOWDOME REVEALS NOTHING. ARRESTS ARE MADE MINOR CHARGES, BUT NONE OF THE STAFF CAN BE LINKED TO THE ROWLEY DEATH.

WE CHECKED OUT THE FISH MEAT SUPPLIER — NOTHING SUSPICIOUS. WE DID TURN UP SOMETHING THOUGH —

— BRIAN ROWLEY TOOK THE INTERCITY ONE-STOP FROM BRIT-CIT VICTORIA YESTERDAY MORNING. HE NEVER PASSED THROUGH CUSTOMS CHECKS ON YOUR SIDE OF THE TUNNEL.

MEKANADROID 30ED JUD

TAK-TIK-TIKKA-TAK

EN THE KILLING PPENED HERE — ATLANTIS.

ATLANTIS
SERVICE
PLEX

DUCT
EXIT

ERIC JECKLE HAD BEEN A MAINTENANCE CHECKER ON THE AT-LANTIC TUNNEL, ATLANTIS SECTION FOR OVER TWENTY YEARS.

IT WAS A LONELY JOB, RIDING THE SEEMINGLY ENDLESS TUNNEL DUCTS. LONELY AND CLAUSTROPHOBIC.

BUT ERIC DIDN'T MIND. HE PREFERRED TO KEEP HIMSELF TO HIMSELF. HE HAD TOO MANY SECRETS THAT MUST NEVER SEE THE LIGHT OF DAY.

AND BESIDES, WORKING THE DUCTS PROVIDED H WITH AN IDEAL METHOD FOR DISPOSING OF BOD

THERE WERE TWO THIS TIME. THE MOST HE AND AUDREY HAD EVER HANDLED WAS A FAMILY OF FIVE. THE SMITHS. THEY'D BEEN ON THEIR WAY TO DO THE GRAND EURO-CIT TOUR.

FIVE PEOPLE AND THEY'D ONLY HAD SEVENTY-NINE CREDS IN CASH! WHAT A FIASCO!

HE LACERATED THE BODIES AND OPENED THE SEA DOOR JUST A CRACK THIS TIME, LETTING THE BLOOD TASTE SEEP OUT INTO THE MURKY DEPTHS. THEY COULDN'T AFFORD ANOTHER MISTAKE LIKE ROWLEY.

ONLY WHEN HE WAS SURE THE **CORAL RAYS** HAD CAUGHT THE SCENT DID HE FULLY OPEN THE WETLOCK—

WATCHED THE FEEDING FRENZY UNTIL THE LAST SCRAP WAS TAKEN.

IT HAD BEEN HIS CARELESSNESS OVER BRIAN ROWLEY THAT HAD LED TO THE BODY BEING FOUND.

STILL, NO MATTER. THERE WAS NO WAY THE JUDGES COULD LINK ROWLEY TO THEM. THEY WERE SAFE.

AUDREY WAS BEING VERY GOOD ABOUT IT, NOT BLAMING HIM — BUT THEY BOTH KNEW IT WAS HIS FAULT.

FORENSIC REPORT ON BRIAN ROWLEY, DREDD.

...VE KEPT ME LOCKED UP IN THIS ROTTEN ...RTMENT FOR **NINE YEARS**! NOW WHEN ...GET OUT I HAVE TO GO IN A ROTTEN ...CASE! WELL I'M NOT DOING IT! I'M **NOT**!

THIS IS SERIOUS, LESLIE.

NO!

YOU WANT US TO GO TO THE **CUBES**, LESLIE? YOU WANT TO END UP ON YOUR **OWN** IN THE **CURSED EARTH**? MMM?

THEY DON'T ALLOW **MUTANTS** IN THE CITIES, YOU KNOW. YOU WANT THAT TO HAPPEN TO YOU?

N-NO...

THEN GET IN THAT CASE, HAIRBAG!

ERIC! THAT'S NOT LIKE YOU!

I...I KNOW. I'M SORRY, AUDREY. IT-IT'S THE PRESSURE.

SOB! SOB!

SORRY, SON. YOU KNOW I DIDN'T MEAN THAT... I LOVE YOU.

ONE OF THE TUNNEL STAFF IS STILL MISSING, DREDD. **ERIC JECKLE**, ONE OF THE CHECKERS.

HE BEEN TOLD?

FOREMAN CALLED HIM IN HALF AN HOUR AGO.

BEEEP BEEP!

COULD BE WE'VE FLUSHED OUT OUR KILLER.

LOOKS LIKE. LET'S GO!

71

THERE IS NO PLACE YOU CAN HIDE. WHEREVER YOU GO, WE'LL TRACK YOU. WHEN YOU SURFACE, YOU WILL BE PICKED UP!
I REPEAT — THERE IS NO ESCAPE!
HE'S RIGHT — WE'RE FINISHED!
OH, ERIC, THIS IS ALL YOUR FAULT!
MY FAULT?
YES! IF YOU'D BEEN MORE CAREFUL ABOUT DISPOSING OF BRIAN—
OH, BRIAN, IS IT? I SHOULD HAVE KNOWN YOU'D BRING THAT UP!
ONE MISTAKE IN NINE YEARS — AND ANYWAY, WHAT ABOUT YOU? WHAT ABOUT YOUR MISTAKES?
ME?
YES! THE SMITHS, FOR INSTANCE! FIVE PEOPLE WE POISONED, AND FOR WHAT? SEVENTY-NINE LOUSY CREDS!
DAD! DAD!
YOU KEEP OUT OF THIS, LESLIE! YOU'RE NOT ENTIRELY BLAMELESS!
OH MY —
NO, DAD! LOOK WHERE YOU'RE GOING!

CRUNCH!

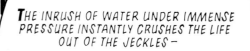

THE INRUSH OF WATER UNDER IMMENSE PRESSURE INSTANTLY CRUSHES THE LIFE OUT OF THE JECKLES —

BLOOD SEEPS INTO THE OCEAN DEPTHS —

—ATTRACTING THE CORAL RAYS.

POOR DEVILS!

IT'S THEIR HOSTAGE I'D WORRY ABOUT.

FOR LITTLE LESLIE, ON HIS FIRST TRIP OUT INTO THE WILD WORLD, THERE IS SADLY NO HAPPY ENDING.

BY THE SOUND OF IT THEY WERE DOING A ROARING TRADE IN STIFFS. LET'S CHECK OUT THEIR APARTMENT.

AUDREY JECKLE'S DIARY REVEALS THE FULL EXTENT OF THE COUPLE'S ACTIVITIES. **SEVENTY-FIVE** POISONINGS OVER NINE YEARS — THE LAST TWO ONLY A FEW HOURS BEFORE...

SHE'D PICK UP THE VICTIMS AT HER WORK, HE'D DISPOSE OF THEM IN ONE OF THE DUCT WETLOCKS. THE PERFECT ARRANGEMENT.

I MAKE IT ALMOST 300,000 CREDS PASSED THROUGH THEIR HANDS — ALL TO PAY THIS DOC DUCKWORTH'S BLACKMAIL DEMANDS. AMAZING!

WHAT'S AMAZING IS SHE WAS DUMB ENOUGH TO KEEP A RECORD OF IT.

SNIFF SNIFF

ONSDALE — GET DOWN TO THE LINIC, PICK UP ONE DOCTOR FRANKLIN DUCKWORTH.

CHARGES?

BLACKMAIL, ACCESSORY TO **SEVENTY-FIVE** COUNTS OF **MURDER**.

AND ALL FOR THE LOVE OF WOLFBOY, HERE.

YEAH, **LOVE**... THERE OUGHTA BE A **LAW** AGAINST IT.

The End

Straitjacket FITS

REAL NAME:	Doctor Drongo Stabbins
RANK/SOCIAL CATEGORY:	Psychiatrist
TIME PERIOD:	2176 AD, Earth
GROUP AFFLIATIONS:	A fellow of the Brilliant Psychiatrists of the World Inc (Human division)
FIRST APPEARANCE:	Judge Dredd The Megazine (Volume 1) 9, "The Straitjacket Fits" (June 1991)
CHARACTER HISTORY:	Doctor Stabbins arrived at the Brit-Cit psycho-cubes with a reputation as the world's greatest psychiatrist. He planned to cure the patients of their range of delusions in just a few sessions, further enhancing his reputation but instead found himself drawn into an increasingly surrealistic web of fantasy and deception. Unknown to Doctor Stabbins, one of the patients had already seized control of the cubes by masquerading as the Chief Robodoc. The patient - Jack - then staged his own escape into a void beyond the panel borders, dragging Doctor Stabbins into his fantasy world...

Straitjacket FITS:
The Final Fit

Writer:	DAVID BISHOP
Artist:	ROGER LANGRIDGE
Lettering:	ROGER LANGRIDGE
Status:	Five years after Doctor Stabbins escaped the clutches of Jack, he returns to the Brit-Cit psycho-cubes to face his ultimate foe!

SORRY I'M LATE. PROBLEMS OUT OF TOWN.

IT'S JACK.

THANK GRUD YOU'RE HERE. THERE'S A **RIOT** GOING ON IN THE BRIT-CIT PSYCHO-CUBES.

THE INMATES TOOK CONTROL THIS MORNING ~ THEY'RE HOLDING NURSE HONEY AND FOUR ROBODOCS **HOSTAGE.**

SORRY TO BRING YOU BACK HERE, BUT THEY DEMAND TO TALK TO **YOU.**

MAR 31

JACK! WHAT DO YOU WANT?

MY DERBY DOCTOR STABBINS, HOW SWEPT OF YOU TO DEMENTIA ME!

I SEE.

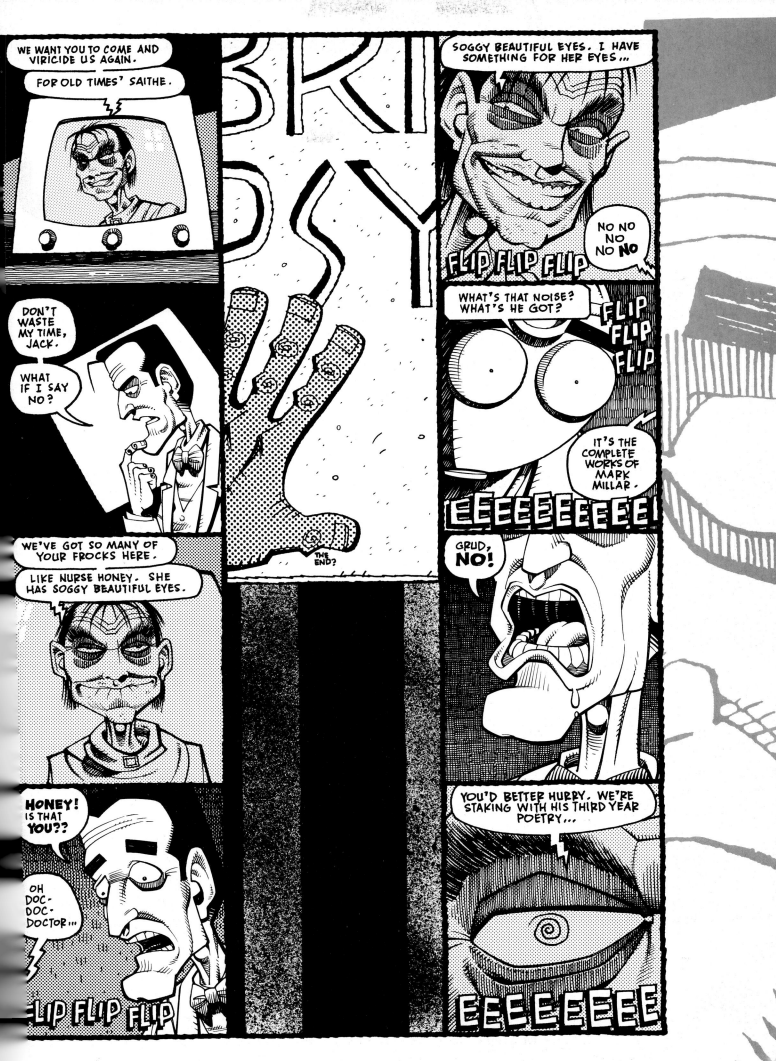

PIN-UP
Brit-Cit Babes
Artwork by Brian Bolland

Judge Joyce

REAL NAME:	Charles Joyce
RANK/SOCIAL	Judge-Sergeant
CATEGORY:	Murphyville, Emerald Isle
BASE OF OPERATIONS:	2114 AD, Earth
TIME PERIOD:	Judge Militia, Emerald Isle
GROUP AFFLIATIONS:	2000 AD Prog 728, "Emerald Isle" Part
FIRST APPEARANCE:	2 (April 1991)
CHARACTER HISTORY:	Young Charlie Joyce wanted to be a judge

Young Charlie Joyce wanted to be a judge ever since his parents were arrested for multiple vehicle theft and grievous assault on a traffic warden. His dream was realised easier than expected on the Emerald Isle, where the Judge Militia more resembles an old fashioned police force than an intensely trained corps of judges. Joyce quickly reached the rank of Judge-Sergeant and in 2110 married his sweetheart Kathleen. He combines an easy-going attitude with a sharp mind and determination to crack any case, as Judge Dredd discovered when they teamed up to fight the Sons of Erin uprising of 2113.

Judge Joyce
When Irish Pies are Smiling

Writer:	GARTH ENNIS
Artist:	STEVE DILLON
Lettering:	GORDON ROBSON
Status:	Judge Joyce stops off at h... bite to eat and uncovers a... of bank robbers, barmy st... body parts!

WRITER: **GARTH ENNIS** · ARTIST: **STEVE DILLON** · LETTERER: **KID ROBSON**

THIS IS JOYCE CALLIN' CONTROL. I'M SIGNIN' OFF FOR HALF AN HOUR, LADS. SEE YEZ.

YOU GOT YOURSELF A BIG WOMAN ON THE SIDE, CHARLIE?

O'DONOGHUES

DROKK OFF, MICK. I'M HAVIN' ME LUNCH.

CHARMIN'! AYE, CONTROL OUT.

GRAND, DAVY. THAT BIG PIE THERE LOOKS IN SEVERE NEED OF BEIN' ATE...

MMMM...

MM-HUH?

PHTOOOO!

THERE'S SOME FELLA IN ME PIE!

JUDGE JOYCE in "WHEN IRISH PIES ARE SMILING!"

Judge Joyce

REAL NAME:	Charles Joyce
RANK/SOCIAL	Judge-Sergeant
CATEGORY:	Murphyville, Emerald Isle
BASE OF OPERATIONS:	2114 AD, Earth
TIME PERIOD:	Judge Militia, Emerald Isle
GROUP AFFLIATIONS:	2000 AD Prog 728, "Emerald Isle" Part
FIRST APPEARANCE:	2 (April 1991)
CHARACTER HISTORY:	Young Charlie Joyce wanted to be a judge

Young Charlie Joyce wanted to be a judge ever since his parents were arrested for multiple vehicle theft and grievous assault on a traffic warden. His dream was realised easier than expected on the Emerald Isle, where the Judge Militia more resembles an old fashioned police force than an intensely trained corps of judges. Joyce quickly reached the rank of Judge-Sergeant and in 2110 married his sweetheart Kathleen. He combines an easy-going attitude with a sharp mind and determination to crack any case, as Judge Dredd discovered when they teamed up to fight the Sons of Erin uprising of 2113.

Judge Joyce
When Irish Pies are Smiling

Writer:	GARTH ENNIS
Artist:	STEVE DILLON
Lettering:	GORDON ROBSON
Status:	Judge Joyce stops off at his local for a bite to eat and uncovers a chef's special of bank robbers, barmy students and body parts!

YOU! YOU'D BETTER HAVE A DROKKIN' GOOD EXPLANATION FOR THIS!

B-B-BUT I DIDN'T KNOW IT WAS LIKE THAT!

RIGHT— WHERE'S YER STOREROOM?

WE GOT 'EM STRAIGHT FROM FINGAL'S FACTORY THIS MORNING, LIKE! WE'VE NEVER HAD TROUBLE WITH THEM BEFORE.

OH AYE?

SYNTH! WHISKEY

FINGAL PIES

FINGAL PIES

OUT

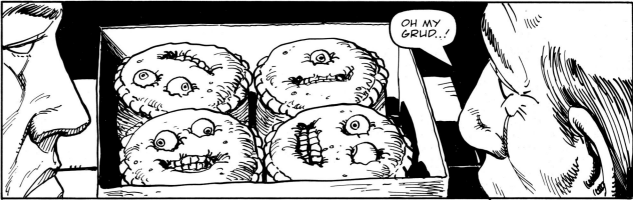

OH MY GRUD..!

HOORRRRP!

I...I HAD A PIE FOR BREAKFAST... OH GRUD...

SOME GET'S GONNA PAY FOR THIS!

I LOVE DOING THE ONES WITH THE FACES, DON'T YOU?

AYE! IMAGINE ALL THE PEOPLE OUT THERE, EATING THESE AND HEAVING THEIR GUTS OUT!

WE'RE SPUGGIN' CRAZY, WE ARE! TOTALLY MAD!

FINGAL'S PIES
FINGAL'S PIES

I THINK WE BETTER GET OUT OF HERE QUIETLY, DOZY...

BOOOAARK!

THEY'VE SEEN US! KILL THEM!

BA-DAMM! BA-DAMM!

AYE, RIGHT!

YEZ ARE ALL UNDER ARREST! *DROP EVERYTHING!!*

STARTIN' WITH *YOU—*

YE HALLION, YE!

AS FOR YOU TWO, DON'T MOVE A DROKKIN' MUSCLE!

WHAT IN *HELL* IS GOIN' ON HERE, ANYWAY?

ER...

WELL...THIS MAY SEEM A WEE BIT *STRANGE...*

IT CERTAINLY DOES —

THE WORLD'S GONE **MAD**...YEZ ARE **MEDICAL STUDENTS** AT TRINITY COLLEGE, YOU GOT GIVEN A **BODY** EACH TO DISSECT, AND YOU THOUGHT IT WOULD BE A GREAT JOKE FOR THE END OF TERM IF YOU BROKE IN HERE AND PUT BITS OF THEM IN THE **PIES**?

WE DIDN'T MEAN ANY HARM, SERGEANT.

AYE...WE **ARE** STUDENTS, AFTER ALL. WE'RE CRAZY AND WHACKY...

WHAT ?!

CRAZY AND WHACKY ? THAT'S A LOAD'VE **DEAD PEOPLE** OVER THERE ! STIFFS ! CORPSES ! AND **YOU** WERE PUTTIN' THEM IN **PIES** FOR A **BIG JOKE** ?!!

I NEARLY ATE ONE O' THE DAMN THINGS MESELF !!

WELL, YEZ MAY BE A COUPLE OF HOTSHOT STUDENTS AT TRINITY—

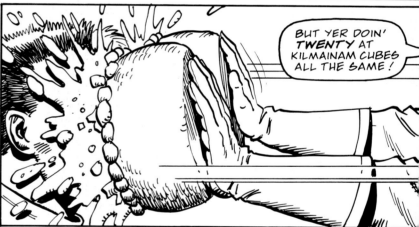

BUT YER DOIN' **TWENTY** AT KILMAINAM CUBES ALL THE SAME !

EAT HUMBLE PIE, YEZ CREEPS !

THE END!

I'M HERE AT THE **STUDE-HABS** FOR **HOTTIE U**, WHERE THE **LATEST** OF THE **RIGHT ARM KILLER'S** VICTIMS HAVE BEEN DISCOVERED.

KEV AND KEVVA ZUSHLAG, THE CARETAKERS OF Z BLOCK, BLASTED OUT OF EXISTENCE WHILE THEY QUIETLY WATCHED THE VID.!

AND UPSTAIRS — IN THE STUDE-HABS THEMSELVES — MORE GRISLY EVIDENCE OF THIS NO DOUBT **RECORD** KILL-FRENZY!

NINETEEN STUDENTS — HANDS THAT WOULD HAVE ONE DAY EXPERTLY FASHIONED THE CITY'S HOTTIES — CUT OFF IN THEIR PRIME!

THIS BRINGS THE KILLER'S TOTAL TO **ONE HUNDRED AND TWENTY FOUR,** ONLY **TEN** SHORT OF THE RECORD!

AND HOW MANY SEVERED LIMBS REMAIN OUT THERE WAITING TO BE DISCOVERED?

ALMOST CERTAINLY MAD TONY NEWTON'S SCORE HAS ALREADY BEEN SMASHED — AND THE **RIGHT HAND KILLER** IS STILL **AT LARGE!**

SOMEONE TELL THEM ABOUT OUR RECORD BREAKER?

HAD TO. COURTESY. HALF THIS INSTALLATION IS THEIR TERRITORY, REMEMBER.

GET READY! HERE IT COMES!

WE'RE SLOWING DOWN! I WARNED YOU—!

IT AIN'T ME! HONEST TA GRUD! THEY CUT THE POWER!

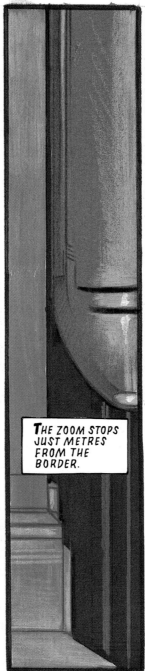

THE ZOOM STOPS JUST METRES FROM THE BORDER.

OUT!

93

YOU MEGA-CITY THICKOS HAVEN'T GOT ME YET! OH, NO, NOT BY LONG CHALKS!

BACK OFF OR THIS ZOOM JOCKEY JOINS THE LIST!

CAN'T GET A CLEAR SHOT AT HIM!

HE'S HEADING FOR THE **BRIT-CIT** SIDE!

I'VE BEATEN YOU! ONCE I'M ON **BRIT-CIT** TERRITORY I'M SAFE!

OH, YOU'LL TRY TO EXTRADITE, OF COURSE, BUT I'LL FIGHT IT! WITH SMART LAWYERS I CAN REMAIN AT LIBERTY FOR YEARS AND YEARS!

FREE AS A BIRD AND **LAUGHING** AT YOU! WORLD RECORD HOLDER!

YOU YANKS, WITH YOUR BIG MOUTHS AND YOUR BRAGGING! WELL, I SHOWED YOU! OH, BY CRIKEY YES! THE PLUCKY LITTLE BRIT PUT ONE OVER ON YOU THIS TIME!

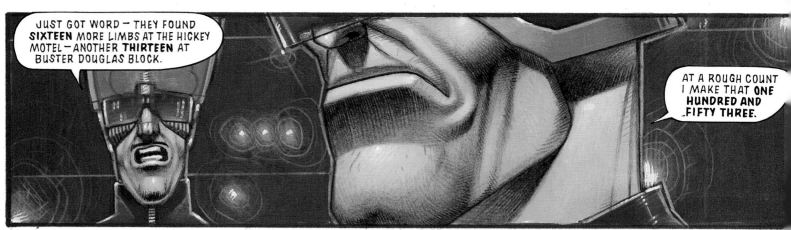

JUST GOT WORD — THEY FOUND **SIXTEEN** MORE LIMBS AT THE HICKEY MOTEL — ANOTHER **THIRTEEN** AT BUSTER DOUGLAS BLOCK.

AT A ROUGH COUNT I MAKE THAT **ONE HUNDRED AND FIFTY THREE.**

YOU'VE GOT TO ADMIT, NOT BAD FOR A BRIT-CIT BOY!

BRIT-CIT! BRIT-CIT!

IF I WAS YOU I WOULDN'T BE CROWING.

ONCE NEWS GETS OUT ABOUT YOUR **BRIT-CIT BOY** YOU'RE GOING TO HAVE HALF THE **CRAZIES** IN MEGA-CITY ONE OVER ON **YOUR** TURF LOOKING FOR **REVENGE** — AND BELIEVE ME, WE GOT A **LOT** MORE CRAZIES THAN YOU.

UH...GOOD POINT!

LISTEN, UH, MAYBE WE COULD JUST **FORGET** THE IDENTITY THING... YOU KNOW, BODY DESTROYED BEYOND RECOGNITION, SOMETHING LIKE THAT?

IT COULD BE ARRANGED, I SUPPOSE PROVIDED OF COURSE THAT BRIT-CI WAS PREPARED TO MAKE A GENEROU DONATION TO THE VICTIMS' SUPPOR FUND...SHALL WE SAY... **200 MILLION?**

TAKE IT OR LEAVE IT.

I SUPPOSE WE'VE NO OPTION.

YOU ARE NOW ENTERING BRIT-CIT TERRITORY

GOOD.

HE'S ALL YOURS THEN.

SEE, CREEP. YOU WERE WRONG. I **DID** TAKE IT AWAY FROM YOU.

NEXT TIME, KEEP 'EM ON YOUR OWN SIDE!